COLLECT MOMENTS NOT THINGS

A TRAVEL JOURNAL

BY SANDRINE KERFANTE

CHRONICLE BOOKS

SAN FRANCISCO

Page 158 constitutes a continuation of the copyright page.

ISBN 978-1-4521-6788-6

Manufactured in China

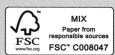

Design by Kayla Ferriera

10 9 8 7 6 5 4 3 2 1

Chronicle Books publishes distinctive books and
gifts. From award-winning children's titles, bestselling
cookbooks, and eclectic pop culture to acclaimed works of
art and design, stationery, and journals, we craft publishing
that's instantly recognizable for its spirit and creativity.
Enjoy our publishing and become part of our community at
www.chroniclebooks.com.

Special quantity discounts are available to corporations and
other organizations. Contact our premiums department at
corporatesales@chroniclebooks.com or at 1-800-759-0190.

Chronicle Books LLC
680 Second Street
San Francisco, California 94107
www.chroniclebooks.com

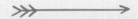

COULDN'T YOU USE A BIT MORE
WONDER IN YOUR LIFE?
A BIT MORE ADVENTURE?

Whether it's nature that calls you or the open road, why not answer? This planet of ours is vast and abundant and filled with magic. There is so much to see and experience. What are you waiting for? You have trails to blaze. You have mountains to climb. You have to walk down forest paths in the afternoon sunlight and stand at the edge of the Grand Canyon and swim in the ocean. So what if it's cold?

Go explore. Challenge yourself. Don't forget how it feels when you reach the summit and look back down at how far you've come. Savor those moments. Keep a record you can return to when you need a reminder of all that you are capable of.

It's easy to fall in love with this world. Just open your eyes. When you leave the lights of the city behind, the night sky looks so much closer to the Earth. If you reach up, you can almost touch the stars.

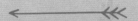

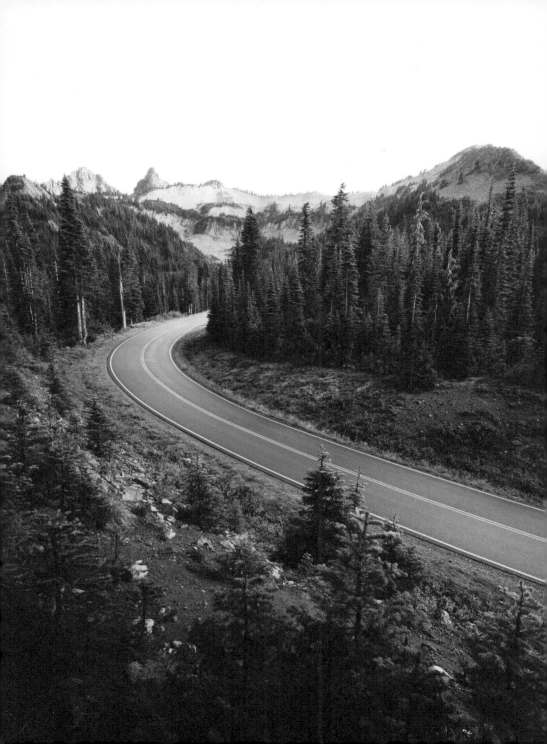

Go
EXPLORE

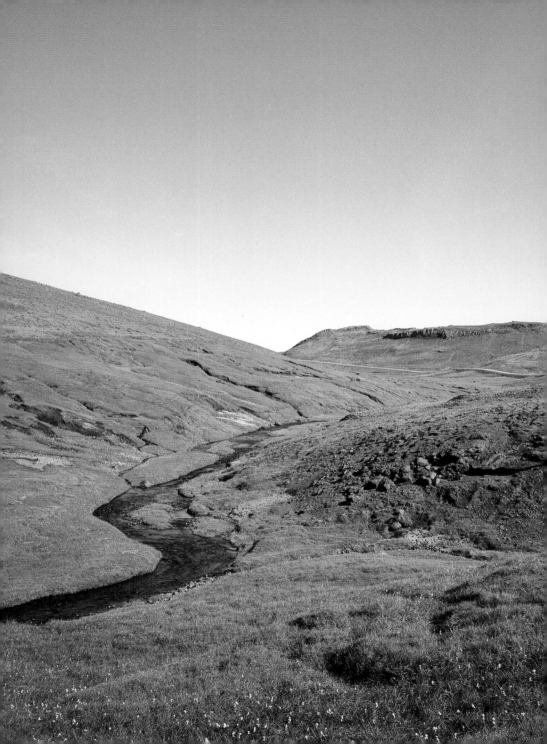

AWAY
FROM THE
CITY

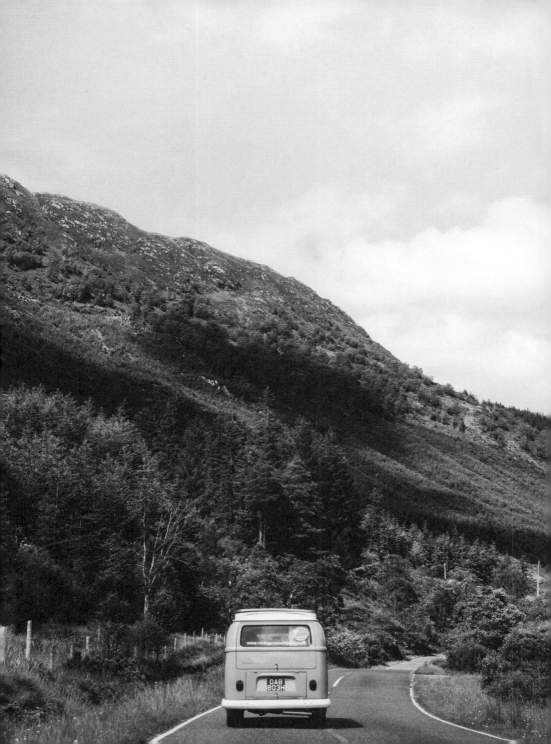

Wild and Free

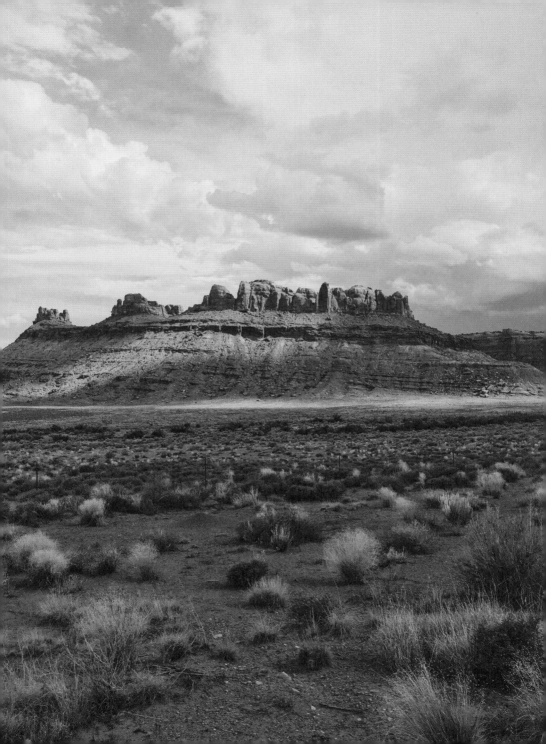

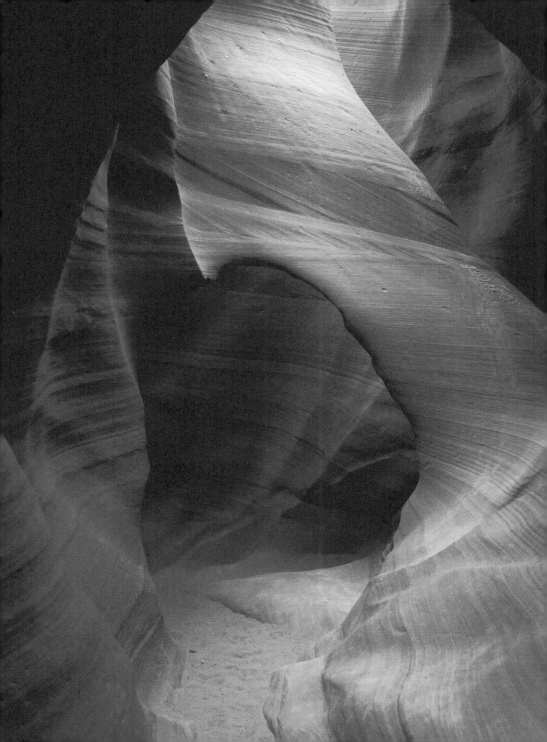

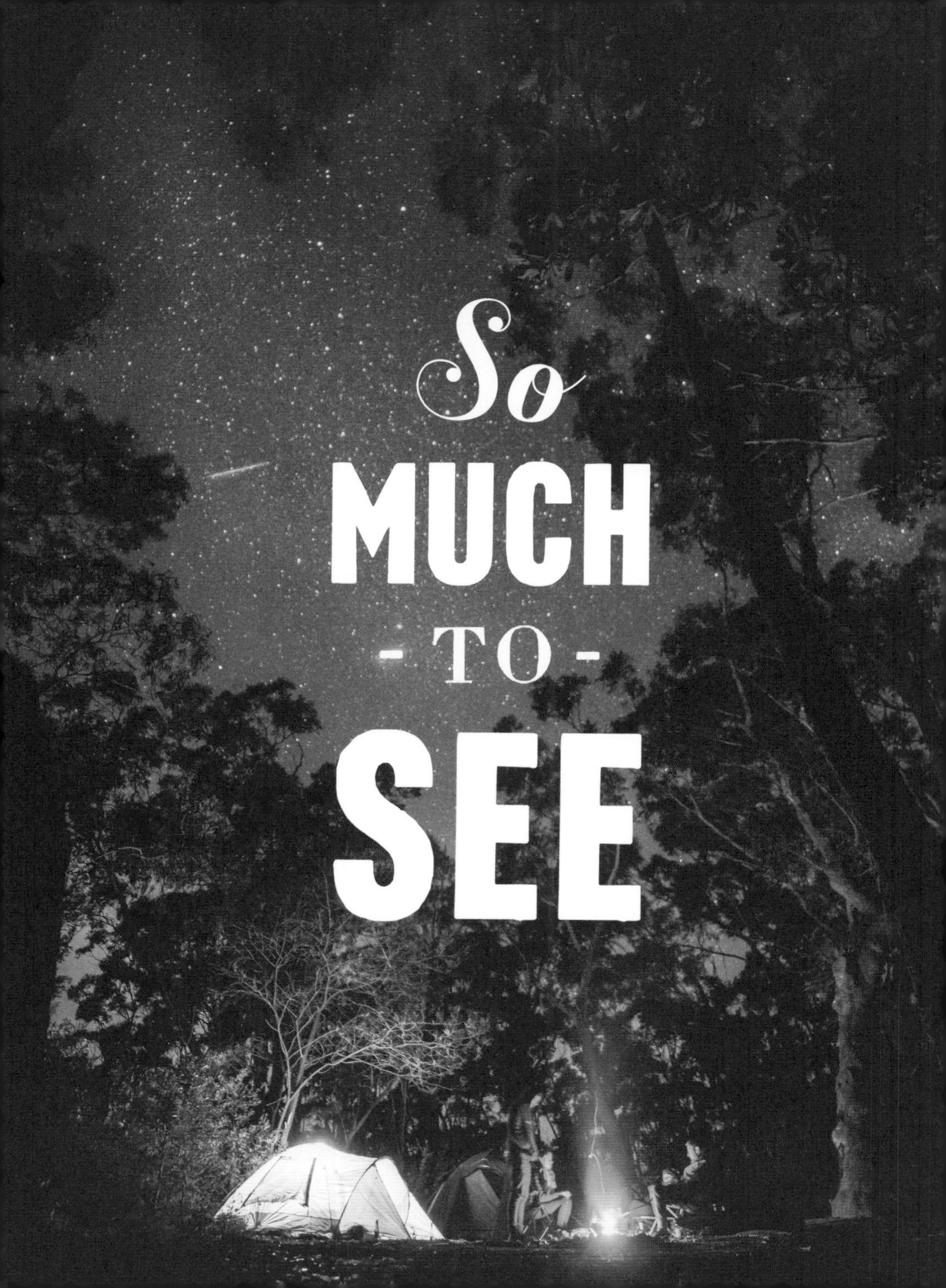
So
MUCH
-TO-
SEE

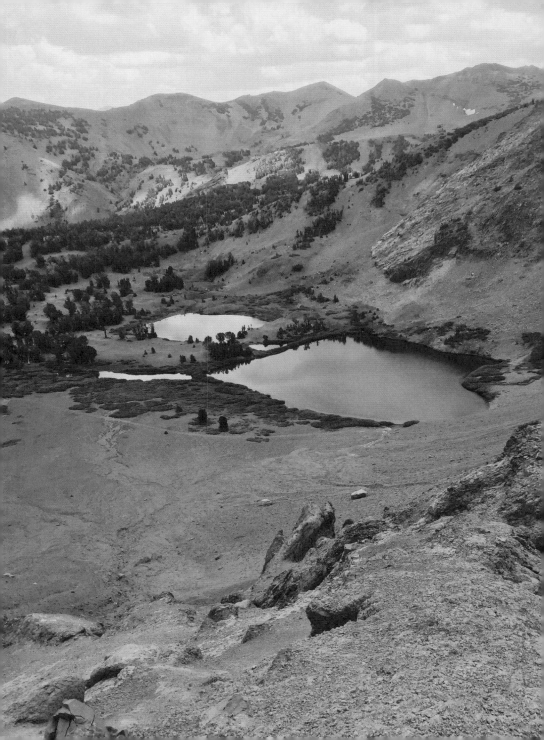

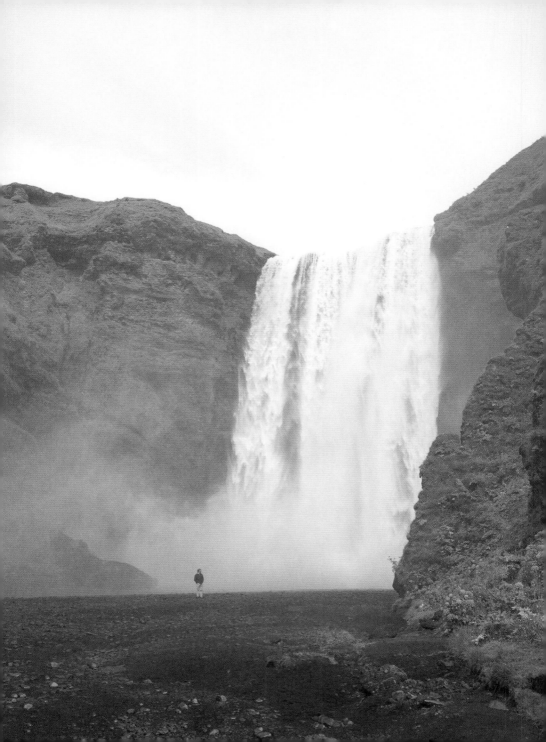

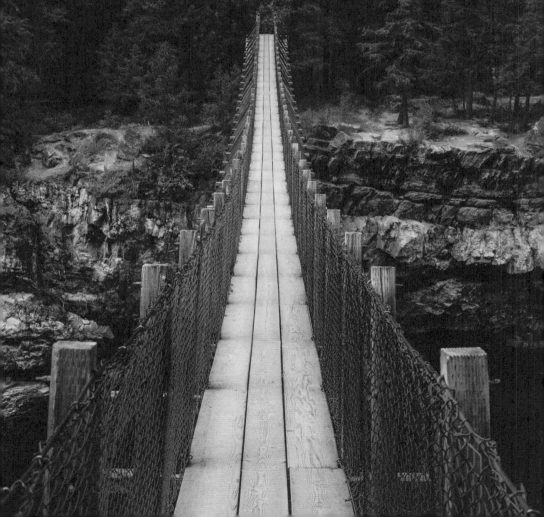

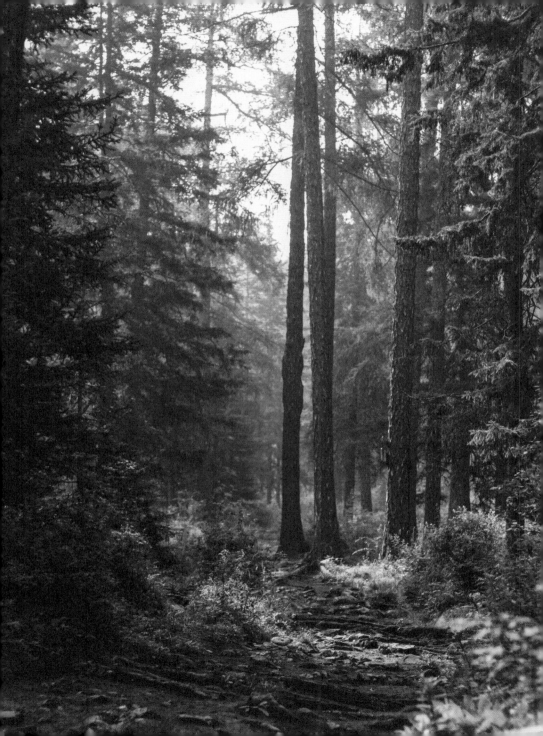

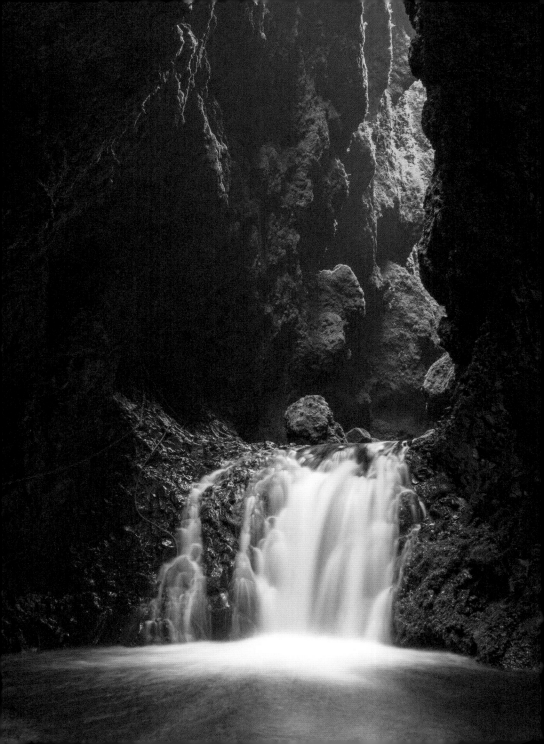

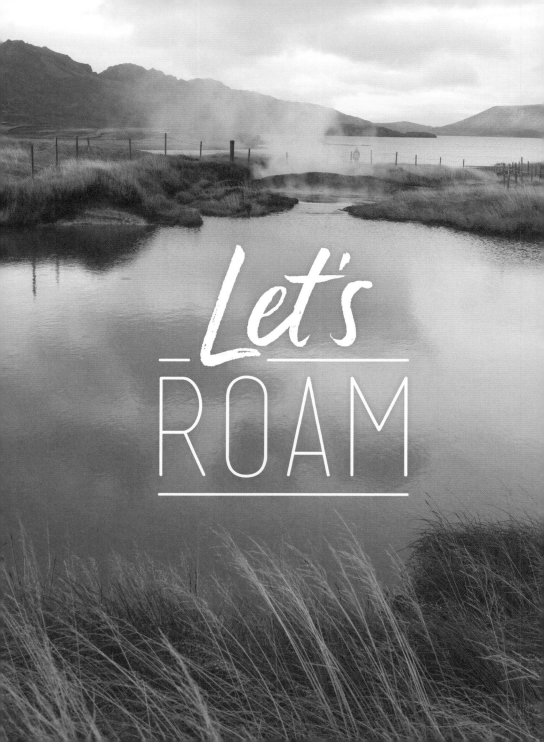

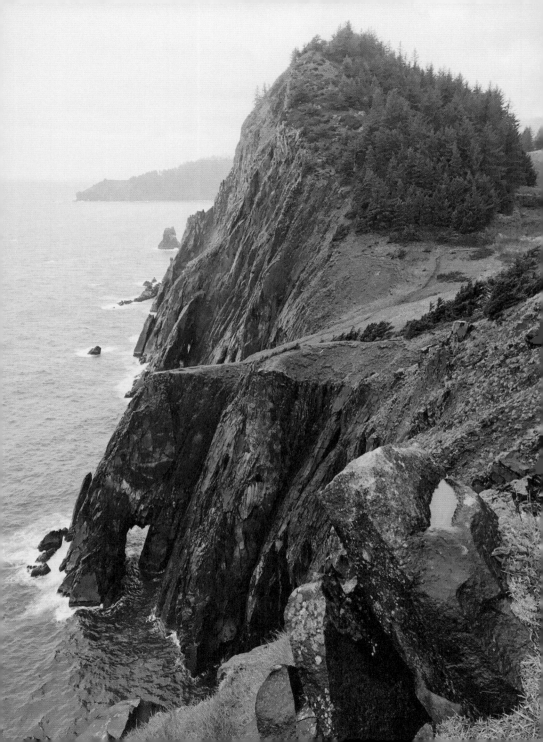

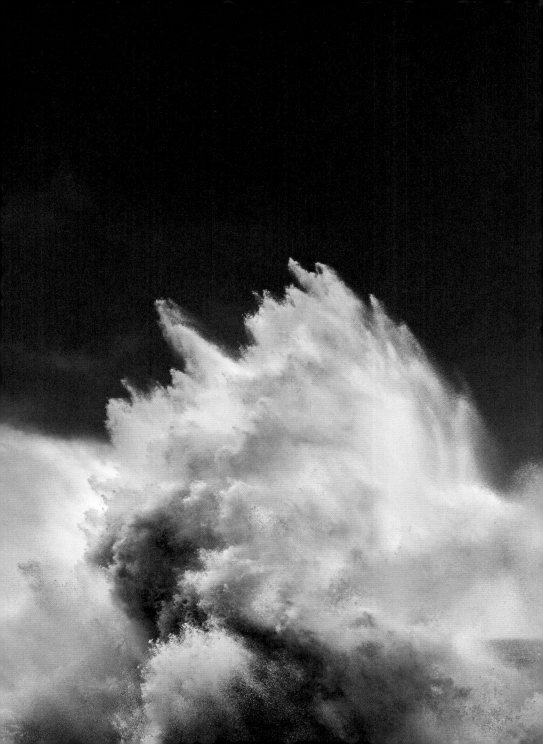

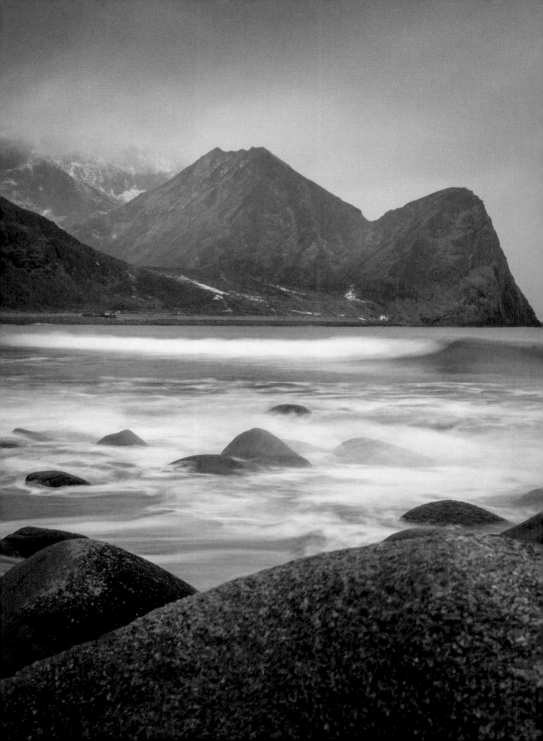

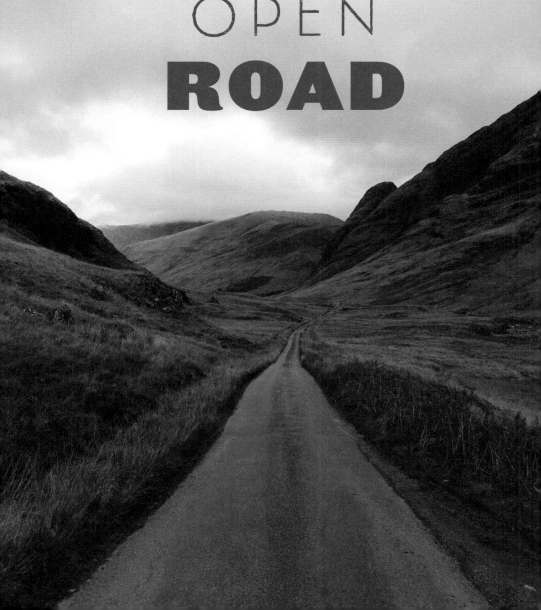

THE
OPEN
ROAD

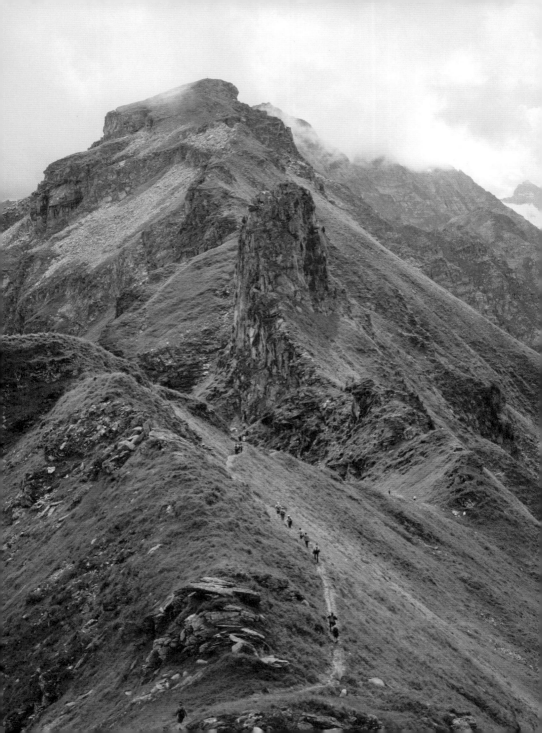

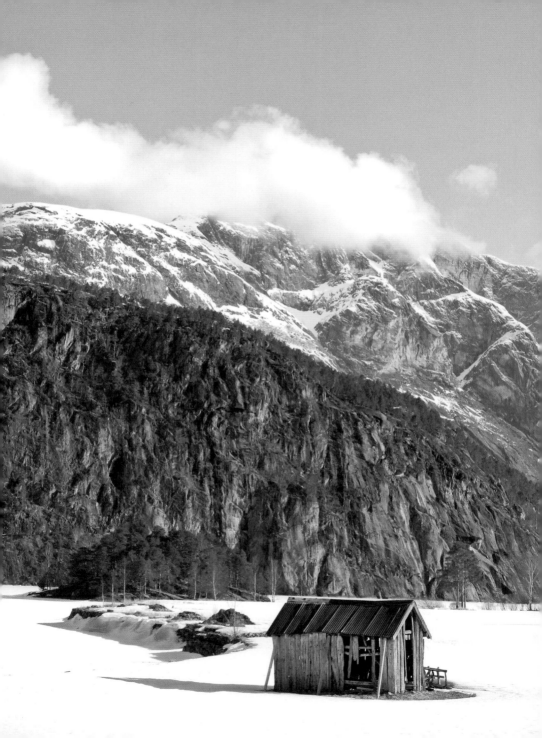

A
Sky
FULL
OF
Stars

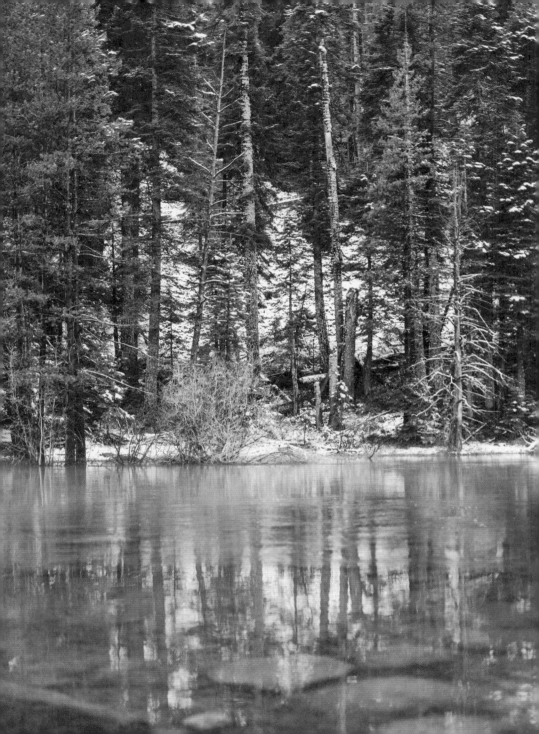

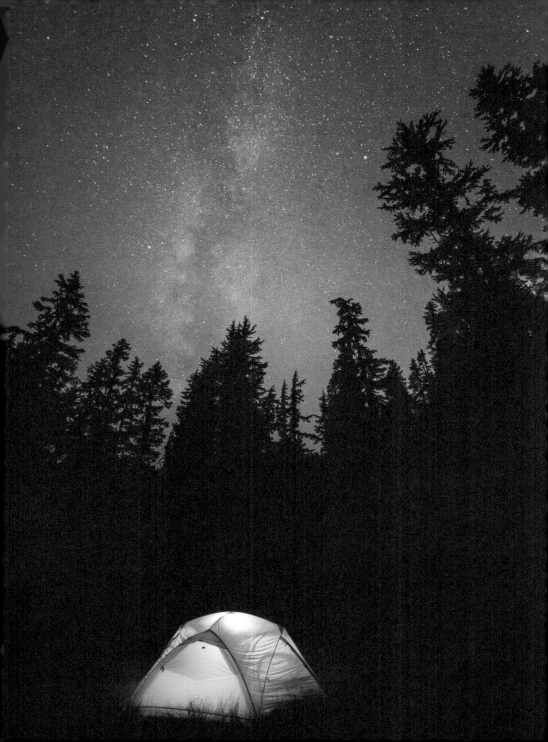

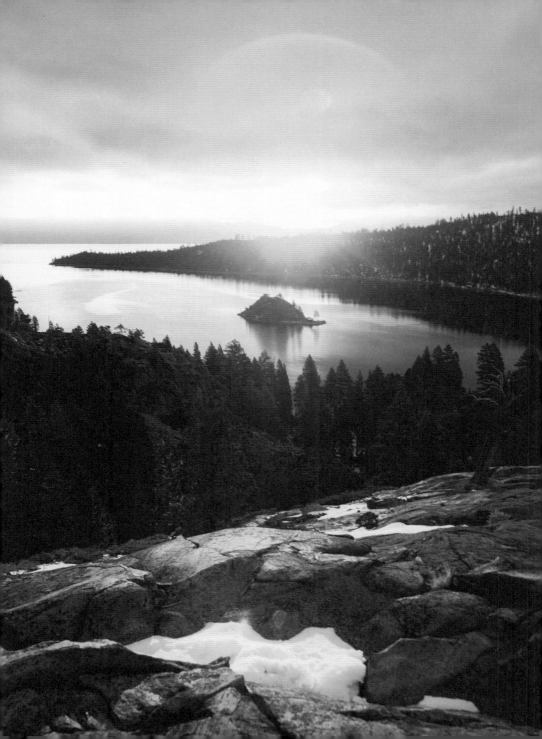

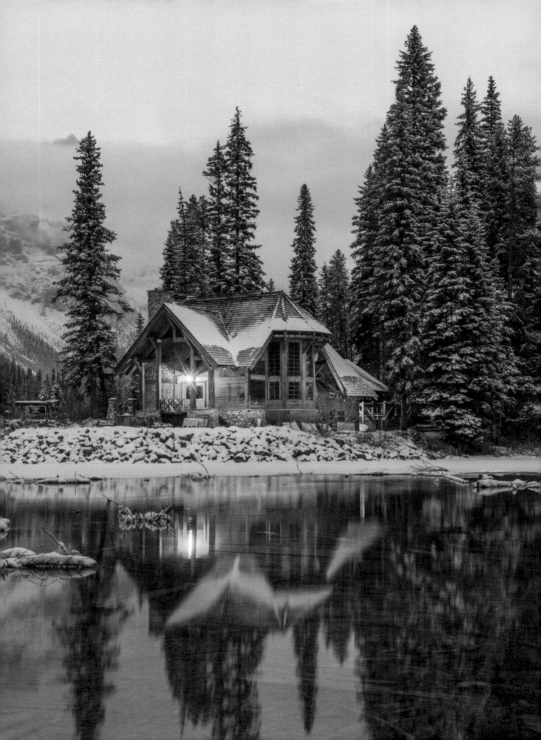

WANDERLUST

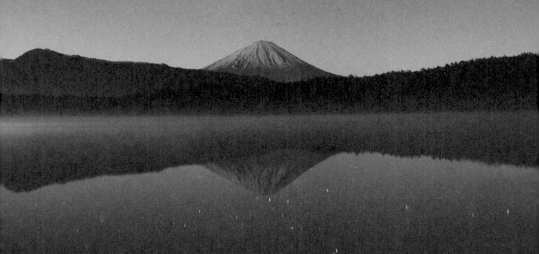

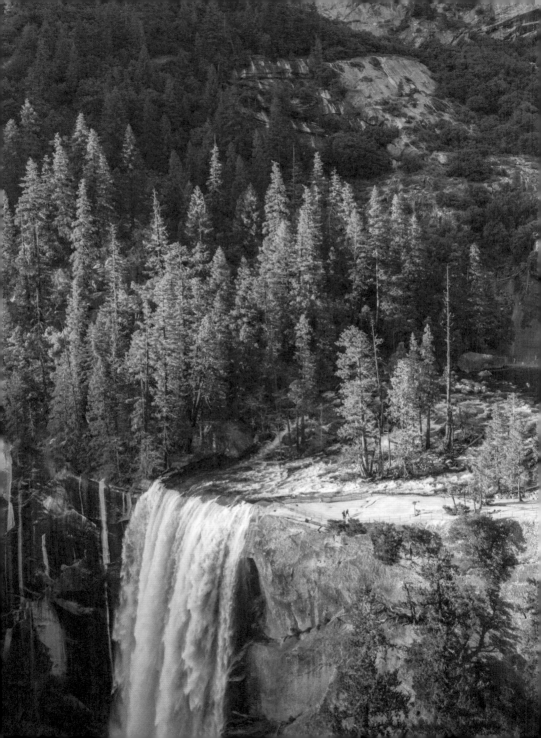

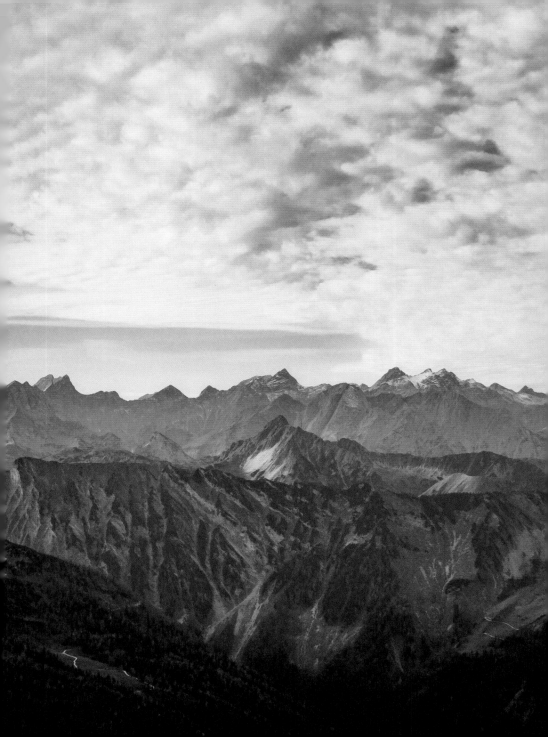

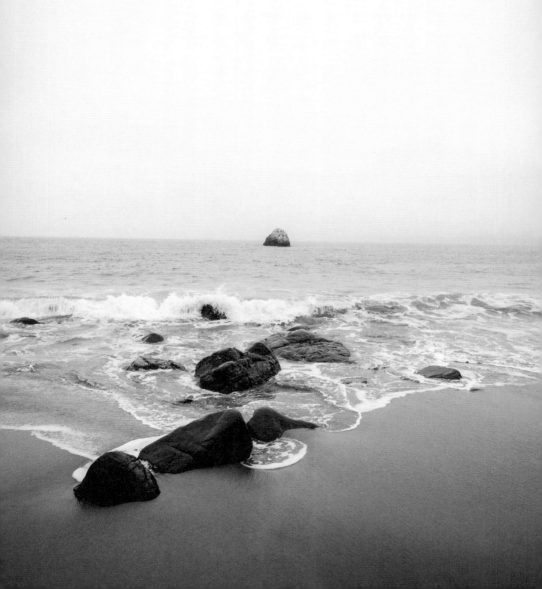

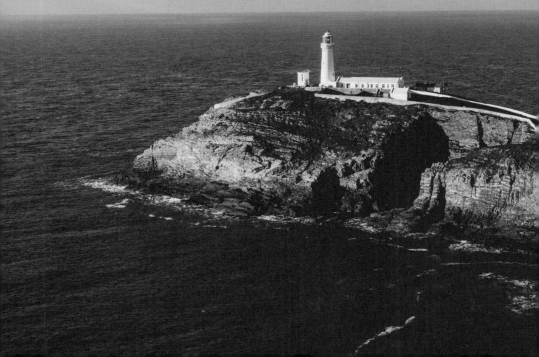

WIND *and* WAVES

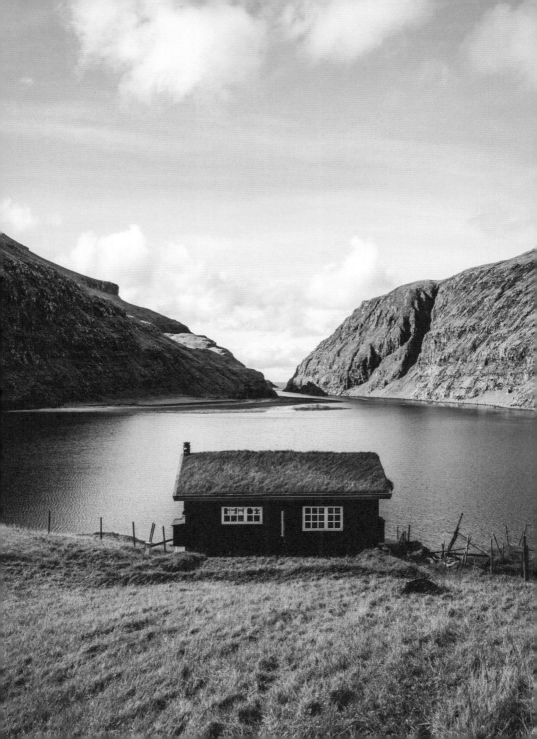

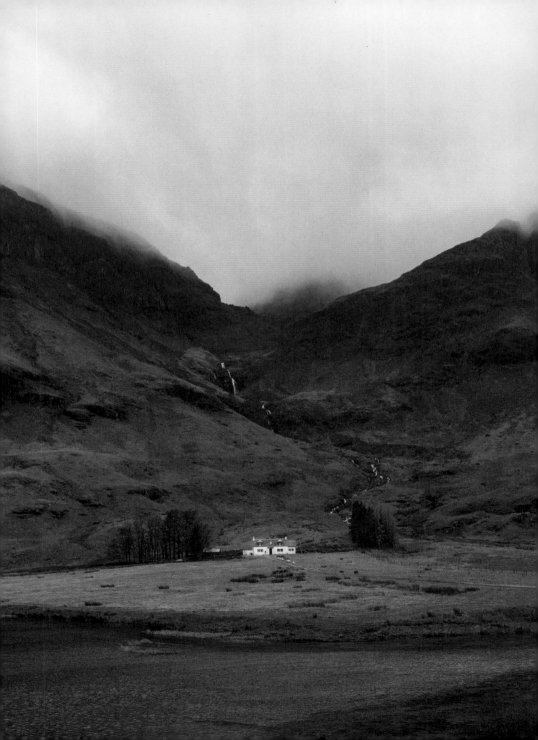

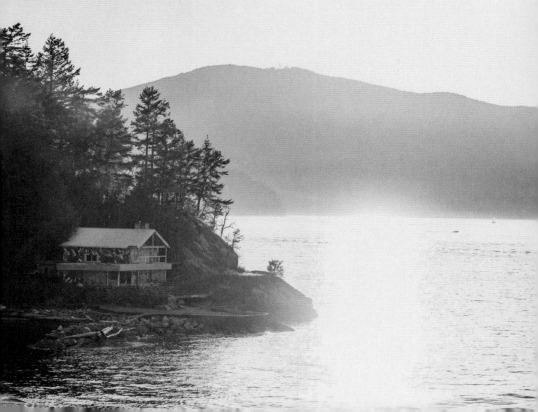

Daydreams AND Sunbeams

CREDITS